New American STREAMLINE

BERNARD HARTLEY & PETER VINEY

CONNECTIONS

An intensive American English series for intermediate students
Workbook A
Units 1–40
REVISED BY TIM FALLA

Oxford University Press

Oxford University Press

198 Madison Avenue
New York, NY 10016 USA

Great Clarendon Street
Oxford OX2 6DP England

Oxford New York

*Athens Auckland Bangkok Bogotá Buenos Aires Cape Town
Chennai Dar es Salaam Delhi Florence Hong Kong
Istanbul Karachi Kolkata Kuala Lumpur Madrid
Melbourne Mexico City Mumbai Nairobi Paris São Paulo
Shanghai Singapore Taipei Tokyo Toronto Warsaw*

*and associated companies in
Berlin Ibadan*

OXFORD is a trademark of Oxford University Press.

ISBN 0-19-434830-X

Based on the American adaptation by Flamm/Northam
Authors and Publishers Services, Inc.

Editor: Ken Mencz
Designer: Arminé Altiparmakian
Senior Art Buyer: Alexandra F. Rockafellar
Picture Researcher: Paul Hahn
Production Manager:

Cover illustration by: Pete Kelly

Illustrations and realia by: Ray Alma, Stephanie Birdsong,
Carlos Castellanos, Dee Deloy, Jenny Dubnau, Maj-Britt
Hagsted, David Hildebrand, Claudia Kehrhahn, Scott
MacNeill, Karen Minot, Tom Powers, Dean Rohrer, VHL
International, William Waitzman, Alina Wilczynski

*The publisher would like to thank the following for their
permission to reproduce photographs:* The Bettman Archive,
Gray Mortimore/Allsport

The publisher would like to thank the following companies:
Boeing, General Motors, Kodak, Sony, Texaco, Viasa
(All brands and product names are registered trademarks of
their respective companies.)

Printing (last digit) 10 9 8 7

Printed in Hong Kong.

TO THE TEACHER

Workbook A of *New American Streamline: Connections* consists of forty units. Each unit relates directly to the corresponding unit in *New American Streamline: Connections*, units 1–40.

The Workbook is an optional component of the series, designed to provide language summaries and additional written exercises. It may be used in the following ways:

1. In more extensive courses as additional classroom material, providing extra oral practice and written reinforcement and consolidation of the basic core material in the Student Book.
2. As homework material in more intensive situations.

The Workbook should only be used after full oral practice of the corresponding unit in the Student Book. The language summaries provide material for review.

Another workbook is available for units 41–80 of the Student Book, under the title Workbook B.

Bernard Hartley
Peter Viney

Unit 1 (Review)

Exercise 1

A. She's from Alabama.
B. *She isn't from Alabama.*
C. *Is she from Alabama?*

Now do the same.

1. A. She comes from Montgomery.

   B. ....

   C. ....

2. A. They've been to Jamaica.

   B. ....

   C. ....

3. A. He works in a bank.

   B. ....

   C. ....

4. A. You're going to Barbados.

   B. ....

   C. ....

5. A. They went to Curaçao.

   B. ....

   C. ....

6. A. There's a shower in the cabin.

   B. ....

   C. ....

Exercise 2

Complete this.

I	me	my	mine
you	....	....	....
....	him	....	....
....	....	her	....
it	....	....	....
....	....	our	....
....	....	....	theirs

Exercise 3

1. *January is the first month.*
2. *February is the second month.*
3. March ....
4. ....
5. ....
6. ....
7. ....
8. ....
9. ....
10. ....
11. ....
12. ....

Exercise 4

Where do you come from?

You're at a party. Complete this conversation. You are B.

A: Hello. What's your name?

B: ....

A: Where do you come from?

B: ....

A: Where's that?

B: ....

A: What do you do?

B: ....

A: Would you like a drink?

B: ....

A: With ice?

B: ....

Unit 2 (Review)

Exercise 1

Look at the first conversation in the Listening Appendix in the Student Book for Unit 2. Write a similar conversation using this information.

Name: Ms. Anita Palacios
Address: 62 Palmer Rd.
                           Duluth
Number: 288-6756
Directory Assistance   Minnesota Telephone

A: Directory Assistance. ....

B: ....

A: ....

B: ....

....

A: ....

....

Exercise 2

Look at the third conversation in the Student Book. You are going to make a collect call to your home, or to a friend's home.
Complete this conversation. You are B.

A: Operator.

B: Hello, ...

A: What name?

B: ....

A: Can you spell that, please?

B: ....

Exercise 3

Match a word from column A with a word from column B.

Column A	Column B
directory	service
extension	assistance
customer	message
collect	relations
area	number
recorded	call
public	code

Exercise 4

Long distance rates to other states

	M	T	W	T	F	S	S
8AM to 5PM	■	■	■	■	■	☐	☐
5PM to 11PM	▨	▨	▨	▨	▨	☐	▨
11PM to 8AM	☐	☐	☐	☐	☐	☐	☐

Dial-Direct	Full Rate Day ■		Evening Discount ▨		Nights & Weekends* ☐	
sample rates from New York City to	First minute	Each additional minute	First minute	Each additional minute	First minute	Each additional minute
Atlanta, GA	1.24	.86	.74	.52	.48	.36
Boston, MA	1.16	.78	.64	.48	.46	.32
Chicago, IL	1.24	.86	.74	.52	.48	.36
Detroit, MI	1.24	.86	.74	.52	.48	.36
Houston, TX	1.28	.88	.76	.54	.50	.36
Los Angeles, CA	1.48	.98	.88	.60	.58	.40
Miami, FL	1.28	.88	.76	.54	.50	.36

*Weekends are Friday 11PM to Sunday 5PM

Look at this information. You are in New York. These are the rates for direct-dialed calls to different cities.
Los Angeles, Tuesday, 11 AM, 6 minutes
$6.38
Now write down the prices of these calls.

1. Chicago, Sunday, 1 PM, 21 minutes

....

2. Detroit, Wednesday, 5:30 PM, 4 minutes

....

3. Atlanta, Friday, 11:20 PM, 9 minutes

....

4. Houston, Sunday, 6:30 PM, 18 minutes

....

5. Boston, Monday, 6:45 AM, 7 minutes

....

6. Miami, Thursday, 3:10 PM, 16 minutes

....

Unit 3 (Review)

Exercise 1

A. I can see some difference.
B. *I can't see any difference.*
C. *Can you see any difference?*

Now do the same.

1. A. He has to do a lot of wash.

   B. ....

   C. ....

2. A. She washed the clothes.

   B. ....

   C. ....

3. A. They've washed the clothes.

   B. ....

   C. ....

4. A. She has some young children.

   B. ....

   C. ....

5. A. They take their clothes to the laundromat.

   B. ....

   C. ....

Exercise 2

white—whiter—whitest

Complete this.

1. soft   ....

2. ....   cleaner   ....

3. ....   better   ....

4. bad   ....

5. ....   more expensive   ....

6. ....   least comfortable

Exercise 3

It's good chocolate. (he) *It's the best chocolate he's ever tasted.*

Continue.

1. It's a good book. (I) ....

2. It's an exciting movie. (they) ....

3. It's a fast car. (she) ....

4. It's a bad movie. (we) ....

5. It's a good detergent. (I) ....

6. It's interesting music. (she) ....

Exercise 4

This is big *but that's bigger.*
These are dirty *but those are dirtier.*

Continue.

1. This is good ....

2. These are bad ....

3. These are interesting ....

4. This is cheap ....

5. This is large ....

6. These are expensive ....

Unit 4 (Review)

Language Summary

I/You He/She We/They	went didn't go did not go	there	yesterday. last week. in 1986. at two o'clock. on Monday.

Did	I/you he/she we/they	go	there?

Yes, I did.
No, she didn't.

I You We They	've have haven't have not	gone.

He She	's has hasn't has not	

Have	I you we they	gone?

Has	he she	

Yes, we have.
No, they haven't.

Yes, he has.
No, she hasn't.

Look at this:

begin—began—begun
crash—crashed—crashed
dive—dived (or dove)—dived
finish—finished—finished
fall—fell—fallen

go—went—gone
get—got—gotten
hit—hit—hit
hold—held—held
hurt—hurt—hurt

jump—jumped—jumped
land—landed—landed
lift—lifted—lifted
make—made—made
run—ran—run

slip—slipped—slipped
swim—swam—swum
throw—threw—thrown
win—won—won

Exercise 1

A. *He swam 100 meters.*
B. *She didn't swim 100 meters.*
C. *Did they swim 100 meters?*
Now do the same.

1. A. He fell.

   B. ....

   C. ....

2. A. ....

   B. She didn't slip.

   C. ....

3. A. ....

   B. She didn't begin it.

   C. ....

4. A. ....

   B. ....

   C. Did they make it?

5. A. ....

   B. ....

   C. Did they finish?

6. A. He won.

   B. ....

   C. ....

Exercise 2

A. *She's begun.*
B. *He hasn't begun.*
C. *Have they begun?*

1. A. ....

   B. ....

   C. Have they fallen?

2. A. She's slipped.

   B. ....

   C. ....

3. A. ....

   B. He hasn't swum 100 meters.

   C. ....

4. A. ....

   B. ....

   C. Have they made it?

5. A. She's finished.

   B. ....

   C. ....

6. A. ....

   B. He hasn't won.

   C. ....

Exercise 3

Women's 100-meter run:
Green   10.58 seconds
Foster   10.55 seconds
Foster ran faster than Green.

Continue.

1. Men's swimming:
   200-meter freestyle.
   Davis   1 minute 51 seconds
   Lopez   1 minute 54 seconds

   ....

   ....

2. Women's running high jump:
   Gold   2.01 meters
   Schmidt   2.00 meters

   ....

   ....

3. Men's 1500-meter run:
   Thomas   3 minutes 35 seconds
   Spolski   3 minutes 36 seconds

   ....

   ....

4. Men's 100-meter run:
   Diaz   9.8 seconds
   Akiyama   9.9 seconds

   ....

   ....

Unit 5 (Review)

Language Summary

I	'll	be	there	tomorrow.		Will	I	be	there?		Yes, I will.
You	will			next week.			you				No, I won't.
He	won't			next year.			he				
She	will not			next month.			she				
It				next Monday.			it				
We				at two o'clock.			we				
They				later.			they				

Exercise 1

he/Tuesday/Sunday
He'll be here next Tuesday, but he won't be here next Sunday.

Continue.

1. I/three o'clock/seven o'clock

....

....

2. she/Wednesday/Saturday

....

....

3. they/week/month

....

....

4. we/later/tomorrow

....

....

5. he/two o'clock/eight o'clock

....

....

6. I/Friday/weekend

....

....

Exercise 2

Reorder the words to make sentences.

time will be what he here?
What time will he be here?

1. won't ten the here train be minutes for.

....

2. it will here be tomorrow?

....

3. he'll the be 7:40 on train.

....

4. in there we'll bookstore be over right the.

....

5. soon it'll here be.

....

6. you will where be?

....

7. I long be won't.

....

8. Monday next here will be Nick.

....

Exercise 3

he/on Wednesday   *Will he be here on Wednesday?*
Continue.

1. they/next week

....

2. it/later

....

3. you/tomorrow

....

4. she/at 4:30

....

Unit 6 (Review)

Exercise 1

Complete this.

Every day...	Yesterday...	Tomorrow...
...she catches the train.	...she caught the train.	...she'll catch the train.
1. ...they get up at seven o'clock.	....	....
2.	...he picked the kids up at school.	....
3.	....	...we'll have dinner at 8:00.
4. ...he meets her at the station.	....	....
5.	....	...he'll read to the kids.
6.	...they watched TV.	....

Exercise 2

I'll walk to school.   *I won't* go to the movies.
Now write true sentences about tomorrow.

1. .... play tennis.

2. .... go to class.

3. .... wash the dishes.

4. .... read a newspaper.

5. .... cook dinner.

6. .... interview Kevin Costner.

7. .... watch television.

8. .... meet the president.

Exercise 3

What *time will she have dinner?* She'll have dinner at seven.

1. Where .... ?

She'll go to New York.

2. Who .... ?

She'll meet Michelle Pfeiffer.

3. What .... ?

They'll play football.

4. When .... ?

He'll take his exams next month.

5. How many .... ?

They'll buy three books.

6. How much .... ?

It'll cost $10,000.

Exercise 4

Will you get up at seven o'clock tomorrow? *Yes, I will.*   Will you have tea with breakfast? *No, I won't.*
Now write true answers.

1. Will you take a bath tomorrow?

....

2. Will you watch television tomorrow?

....

3. Will you interview Tom Cruise?

....

4. Will you come to class on Saturday?

....

5. Will you do the wash today?

....

6. Will you take a bus home tomorrow?

....

Unit 7 (Review)

Language Summary

Future with *will* (continued)

Exercise 1

Laura lives in New York. She's going on vacation to Hawaii.

She won't need to take a coat.

She'll need to take a swimsuit.

1. ....

2. ....

3. ....

4. ....

5. ....

6. ....

Exercise 2

Dr. Sowanso is the Secretary General of the United Nations. He's one of the busiest men in the world. This is his itinerary for August.

Aug. 10 Berlin/Germany/Chancellor/Europe
Aug. 13 Nairobi/Kenya/President/Africa
Aug. 17 Riyadh/Saudi Arabia/King/Middle East
Aug. 22 Tokyo/Japan/Prime Minister/Asia
Aug. 25 Ottawa/Canada/Prime Minister/North America
Aug. 31 Brasilia/Brazil/President/South America

On August 10, he'll be in Berlin. He'll meet the German Chancellor. They'll discuss European affairs.

Now describe the rest of his trip.

1. ....
....
....

2. ....
....
....

3. ....
....
....

4. ....
....
....

5. ....
....
....

Exercise 3

Will Dr. Sowanso visit Berlin? Yes, he will.
Will he visit London? No, he won't.

1. Will he visit Mexico City?

....

2. Will he visit Ottawa?

....

3. Will he visit Riyadh?

....

4. Will he visit Melbourne?

....

5. Will he visit Madrid?

....

Unit 8 (Review)

Language Summary

I	was	sleeping.
He/she		
We/you/they	were	

Was	I	sleeping?
	he/she	
Were	you/we/they	

Yes, he was.
No, she wasn't.

Yes, you were.
No, we weren't.

Have	I/you/we/they	ever had a nightmare?
Has	he/she	

Yes, I have.
No, he hasn't.

Look at this:

dream—dreamed—dreamed   stand—stood—stood   feed—fed—fed
get up—got up—gotten up   sleep—slept—slept   meet—met—met

Exercise 1

Complete these.

1. need ....
2. .... began ....
3. .... hurt
4. swim ....
5. .... stood
6. sleep ....
7. .... fed ....
8. .... thrown
9. .... fallen
10. eat ....

Exercise 2

Make sentences.

I/woke/flight attendant/shake my arm
When I woke, the flight attendant was shaking my arm.

1. I/woke/teacher/call my name

   ....

2. I/woke/my sister/walk/out of our room

   ....

3. I/woke/fire fighter/climb/into the room

   ....

4. I/woke/a man/stand/near the door

   ....

Exercise 3

Make questions.

accident/happen
What were you doing when the accident happened?

1. letter/arrive

   ....

2. president/give his speech

   ....

3. phone/ring

   ....

4. I/be in Los Angeles

   ....

Exercise 4

Answer these questions.

1. How many hours of sleep do you need?

   ....

2. What time do you usually go to bed?

   ....

3. What time do you usually get up?

   ....

4. What time did you go to bed last night?

   ....

5. What time did you get up this morning?

   ....

6. Did you sleep well or badly last night?

   ....

7. Have you ever walked in your sleep?

   ....

8. Have you ever had a nightmare?

   ....

Unit 9

Language Summary

Can I help you?
Could I have a box of throat lozenges, please?

Could you fill this prescription?
Should I pay now or later?

Look at this:

pills

tablets

capsules

throat lozenges

Exercise 1

Look at the first conversation in the Student Book. Write a similar conversation using these words: bad sore throat/ a couple of days/these throat lozenges/two/twice a day.

A: Can I help you?

B: ....

A: ....

B: ....

A: ....
....

B: ....

A: ....

Exercise 2

Put the sentences in the correct order to make a conversation.

☐ Without.

☐ There you go. Will that be all?

☐ Could I have a tube of toothpaste, please?

☐ That's OK. Here's your change.

☐ Yes, that's all. Sorry, I only have a hundred-dollar bill.

☐ With fluoride or without?

Exercise 3

pay now/later   *Should I pay now or later?*

Continue.

1. do it tomorrow/the day after tomorrow

....

2. give it to you at lunchtime/this afternoon

....

3. finish it now/in a few minutes

....

4. go now/at three o'clock

....

Exercise 4

Look at the third conversation.

hair gel

chocolate

potato chips

roll of film

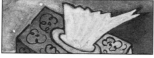
tissues

bandages

shaving cream

shampoo

Could I have a tube of hair gel, please?

Write sentences.

1. ....

2. ....

3. ....

4. ....

5. ....

6. ....

7. ....

Unit 10

Language Summary

I/You We/They	want don't want	it. them.
He She	wants doesn't want	her. him.

I You We They	want don't want	me you him her it	to	do that. see them. meet him. talk to her.
He She	wants doesn't want	us them		

I/You We/They	want don't want	to	do that. see them.
He She	wants doesn't want		talk to her. meet him.

What Who	do you want?
What	do you want to do?
What	do you want her to do?

Exercise 1

Pam Adams is a race car driver. She's talking to a reporter at the beginning of the new car-racing season. "I want to win this race. I want to be the fastest and best driver. I want to be the world champion. I want to retire after this season. I don't want to race next year. I want to watch the races on TV!"

She wants to win this race.

Write five sentences.

1. ....
2. ....
3. ....
4. ....
5. ....

Exercise 2

Thomas B. Worthington is a businessman. He wants his staff to do several things today. He's made a list.

Laura (accountant)

Harry (administrative assistant)

Howard and Lucy (typists)

read special report discuss report with Harry make some calls write summary of report	order lunch reserve table at Lutece's restaurant pick up theater tickets book a flight to London	type some letters type special report photocopy special report give copies to Harry

Laura: *He wants her to read the special report.*
Harry: *He wants him to order lunch.*
Howard and Lucy: *He wants them to type some letters.*

Now write three sentences about Laura, about Harry, and about Howard and Lucy.

Laura

1. ....

....

2. ....

....

3. ....

....

Harry

1. ....

....

2. ....

....

3. ....

....

Howard and Lucy

1. ....

....

2. ....

....

3. ....

....

Unit 11

Language Summary

It	looks	good.		They	look	good.		It looks like a used car.
	feels				feel			They feel like fur.
	tastes				taste			It tastes like an apple.
	sounds				sound			It sounds like a train.
	smells				smell			It smells like coffee.

Exercise 1

sweet   sour
rich   poor

Now write the opposites. Use these words:
expensive/stale/boring/thin/easy/old/ unhappy/beautiful/light/right/soft/strong/ uncomfortable/clean/cool/dry/cold/ fast/short.

1. cheap ....
2. comfortable ....
3. warm ....

4. hot ....
5. fresh ....
6. happy ....
7. interesting..................................
8. new..
9. left ....
10. hard ....
11. weak...

12. tall...
13. ugly...
14. dirty ....
15. difficult ....
16. wet..
17. slow ....
18. heavy...
19. thick...

Exercise 2

Pierre Lebrun/French/Canada

A: *Your name sounds French.*
B: *Yes, but I'm not French. I'm from Canada.*

Continue.

1. Miguel Gonzales/Spanish/the United States

    A: ....
    B: ....

2. John Smith/English/Australia

    A: ....
    B: ....

3. Fritz Schmidt/German/Austria

    A: ....
    B: ....

4. Luigi Gordini/Italian/Switzerland

    A: ....
    B: ....

Exercise 3

This perfume's nice.   *Yes, it smells nice.*
This room's warm.   *Yes, it feels warm.*

Continue.

1. This steak is excellent.

    ....

2. That house is modern.

    ....

3. These vegetables are fresh.

    ....

4. That radiator's hot.

    ....

5. This coat's expensive.

    ....

6. This cheese is awful.

    ....

Exercise 4

smell/coffee
What does it smell like?
It smells like coffee.

1. look/leather

    ....
    ....

2. taste/milk

    ....
    ....

3. smell/cheese

    ....
    ....

4. feel/glass

    ....
    ....

5. sound/jazz

    ....
    ....

Unit 12 (Review)

Look at this:

fly—flew—flown
say—said—said
put—put—put

understand—understood—understood
stick—stuck—stuck
switch—switched—switched

breath—breathed—breathed
reply—replied—replied
step—stepped—stepped

Exercise 1

Complete these.

1. is ....

2. .... were ....

3. hit ....

4. .... stood ....

5. take off ....

6. .... put on ....

7. stop ....

8. carry ....

9. descend ....

10. .... snored ....

11. use ....

12. .... said

Exercise 2

"We can't see the surface of the planet."
They couldn't see the surface of the planet.

Continue.

1. "We can breathe the air."

....

2. "We can't find any intelligent life."

....

3. "We can't start the engines."

....

4. "We can't take off."

....

5. "We can take off our helmets."

....

Exercise 3

Complete these.

something	anything	nothing	everything
1.	anywhere	....	....
2.	....	no one	....
3.	....	....	everybody
4. some	....	....	....

Exercise 4

white clouds   *There were too many white clouds.*
noise   *There was too much noise.*

Continue.

1. people

....

2. traffic

....

3. cars

....

4. buses

....

5. pollution

....

6. smoke

....

Unit 13

Language Summary

It's too hot for me to drink.
It's cool enough for me to drink.
I'm not strong enough to lift it.
She isn't old enough to get married.

catch—caught—caught
forget—forgot—forgotten
leave—left—left
bring—brought—brought

Exercise 1

It's very hot. I can't drink it.   *It's too hot for me to drink.*
Continue.

1. It's very expensive. We can't buy it.

....

2. It's very heavy. They can't carry it.

....

3. It's very high. He can't touch it.

....

4. It's very sweet. She can't drink it.

....

5. It's very far. I can't walk there.

....

6. It's very quiet. You can't hear it.

....

Exercise 2

They're cheap. I can buy them.
They're cheap enough for me to buy.
Continue.

1. It's loud. They can hear it.

....

2. It's easy. We can understand it.

....

3. They're light. He can lift them.

....

4. It's cool. They can drink it.

....

5. It's easy. You can do it.

....

6. They're good. I can use them.

....

Exercise 3

We can't buy it. We aren't rich enough.   *We aren't rich enough to buy it.*
Continue.

1. She can't carry them. She isn't strong enough.

....

2. He can't drive. He isn't old enough.

....

3. He can't lift them. He isn't strong enough.

....

4. They can't sleep. They aren't tired enough.

....

5. I can't eat. I'm not hungry enough.

....

6. You can't play professional football. You aren't good enough.

....

Exercise 4

I can't vote. I'm too young.   *I'm too young to vote.*
Continue.

1. She can't get married. She's too young.

....

2. He can't help us. He's too busy.

....

3. They can't work. They're too tired.

....

4. I can't stay here. I'm too cold.

....

Unit 14

Language Summary

I/You He/She We/They	could couldn't could not	go out. see it.	I/You He/She We/They	wanted to didn't want to did not want to	go out. see it.	I/You He/She We/They	had to didn't have to did not have to	go out. see it.

Exercise 1

She wanted to go out but she couldn't. She had to stay home.

Continue.

1. ....
....
....

2. ....
....
....

3. ....
....
....

4. ....
....
....

Exercise 2

I can't help you with your homework.
Why can't you help me with my homework?

Continue.

1. They couldn't come last night.

   ....

2. I didn't want to go out.

   ....

3. He didn't have to go to work yesterday.

   ....

4. I haven't been to work today.

   ....

5. She's not listening to him.

   ....

6. They can't bring it.

   ....

7. I can't see you tomorrow.

   ....

8. He doesn't have a pen.

   ....

9. She doesn't like him.

   ....

10. I won't be here tomorrow.

   ....

Unit 15

Language Summary

I/You He/She We/They	'll will won't will not	have to	wear a uniform.		Will	I/you he/she we/they	have to	wear a uniform?
I You We They	've have haven't have never	had to	wear a uniform.		Have	I you we they	ever had to	wear a uniform?
He She	's has hasn't has never				Has	he she		

Exercise 1

	Robert	Cathy	Pamela and Andrew
wear a uniform	✔	✔	✗
work at night	✔	✔	✗
pass an exam	✔	✔	✔
drive a car	✗	✔	✗
correct homework	✗	✗	✔
give shots	✔	✗	✗
write reports	✔	✔	✔

Write sentences about Robert, Cathy, and Pamela and Andrew.

Robert

He'll have to give shots.

1. ....
2. ....
3. ....
4. ....
5. ....
6. ....

Cathy

She won't have to give shots.

1. ....
2. ....
3. ....
4. ....
5. ....
6. ....

Pamela and Andrew

They won't have to give shots.

1. ....
2. ....
3. ....
4. ....
5. ....
6. ....

Exercise 2

Amelia is a princess. When she was ten her father died, and she inherited $30,000,000!

work   *She's never had to work in her life.*

Write five sentences. You can use these words: worry about money/wash dishes/iron a blouse/cook a meal/get up early.

1. ....
2. ....
3. ....
4. ....
5. ....

Unit 16

Language Summary

I You We They	've have haven't have not	been able to	work	for two days. since last Tuesday.
He She	's has hasn't has not			

I can swim now. I could swim when I was five. } I'm able to swim now. I was able to swim when I was five. }

I've been able to swim since I was five. I've been able to swim for a long time.

Exercise 1

Put these words in the correct place.

Tuesday	January 12
five minutes	ten o'clock
8:42	ten years
two weeks	March
two hours	six weeks
four weeks	last spring
I was young	eight years
a long time	last week
1989	a couple of days

for	since
two years	1993
....	....
....	....
....	....
....	....
....	....
....	....
....	....
....	....

Exercise 2

A. she/play tennis/Friday
She hasn't been able to play tennis since Friday.

B. she/go outside/two days
She hasn't been able to go outside for two days.

Continue.

1. A. he/talk/a week

....

B. he/call his mother/Saturday

....

2. A. she/play the piano/a long time

....

B. she/use her hand/last month

....

3. A. they/walk/the accident

....

B. they/play football/two weeks

....

4. A. we/clean our room/last weekend

....

B. we/sleep/three nights

....

Unit 17

Language Summary

I	'll	be able to	go.		Will	I	be able to	go?	Yes, I will./No, I won't.
You	will					you			Yes, he will./No, he won't.
He	won't					he			
She	will not					she			
We						we			
They						they			

Exercise 1

Look at the first conversation in the Student Book. You are making a change. Complete this conversation with this information: last week/my family/accountant.

A: Why do you want to study accounting?

B: ....

....

A: Uh-huh. Do you have enough money to take the course?

B: ....

....

A: Fine. The course costs $3,000.

B: ....

....

A: Of course! Just sign here.

Exercise 2

Look at the third conversation in the Student Book. You want to make a change. Complete this conversation with this information: the Canadian office/Montreal or Quebec/French/problems with my feet.

A: Have a seat. You work in accounting, right?

B: ....

....

A: Why do you want to work for the Canadian office?

B: ....

....

A: Uh-huh. How good is your French?

B: ....

....

A: So what will you be able to do for the Canadian office?

B: ....

....

Exercise 3

Will you be able to come to my party? [✗] *No, I won't.*   Will you be able to drive me to the airport? [✔] *Yes, I will.*
Continue.

1. Will you be able to help me? [✔]

....

2. Will you be able to work on Saturday? [✗]

....

3. Will you be able to see him next week? [✗]

....

4. Will you be able to meet him at 10:30? [✔]

....

Exercise 4

Would you like to go to the movies on Saturday? (wash my hair)   *I'm sorry, I won't be able to. I'm washing my hair.*
Continue.

1. Would you like to play tennis tomorrow morning? (work)

....

2. Would you like to go out for dinner tonight? (go to the opera)

....

3. Would you like to come shopping with me? (take the dog for a walk)

....

4. Would you like to go for a walk in the park this afternoon? (clean my house)

....

5. Would you like to go to the theater tomorrow? (go out for dinner with Sue)

....

6. Would you like to go on vacation with me this summer? (go with Kevin)

....

Unit 18

```
~~~~~~~~~~~~~~~~~~~~~~
    SUPERFOODS, INC.
  STORE #16         8/17/95

Cookies                2.49
Cornflakes 500g        4.29
  (17.65 oz)
Butter 500g (17.65 oz) 2.99
Milk 21                2.34
Apples 1.5kg           1.34
Rice 1kg               2.74
Sweet corn (can)        .89
Frozen pizzas          4.49

TOTAL                 21.57
CHECK                 21.57
CHANGE                  .00
```

```
WILLIAM T. RIVERS                                   787
1099 BANK ST.
NEW YORK, NY 10014          Oct. 13 19 95      51-32
                                                211
PAY TO THE   Superfoods              $  21.57
ORDER OF
Twenty-One and 57/100 ———————————— DOLLARS

FIRST NATIONAL BANK
112 Third Avenue New York, NY 10003
            Groceries              William T. Rivers
MEMO
:021800329: 48 01 939 3782
```

Now complete these checks.

1000 ADDRESS LABELS FOR ONLY **$3.99**

MRS. THOMAS A. MOORE
431 BRIAR ROAD NE
GRAND RAPIDS, MI 49503

Actual size

[ ] 1000 Adhesive Address Labels $3.99
[✓] 500 Peel-Off Address Labels $6.99
[ ] 500 Christmas Address Labels $5.99

Name Hector Arroyo
Street 319 West 14th St. Apt. 3-A
City New York   State NY   ZIP 10014

Send check or money order. Add 50¢ for postage and handling.
Allow 4–6 weeks for delivery. Mail to:
Addressograph, Box 1721, Liverpool, NY 13088

```
HECTOR ARROYO                                       77
319 W. 14TH STREET
NEW YORK, NY 10014          _____ 19___   51-7212
                                                9332
PAY TO THE
ORDER OF _____  $_____

_____ DOLLARS

MERCHANT'S BANK OF NEW YORK
200 MADISON AVENUE NEW YORK, NY 10016

MEMO _____
:246546449: 26 53 43435343 1475
```

QUARTZ KLOX

BOX 307, FAIR OAKS, CA 95628

Please send me:
_3_ "Stick-Up" Digital Clocks @ $4.29 each
____ Digital Clocks/Ballpoint Pens @ $9.49 each
_2_ Digital Clocks/Pendants @ $7.29 each

Add $4.50 for shipping. Send check or money order only.
Do not send cash. Allow 6 weeks for delivery.

Please print.
Name: Susan Yamamoto
Address: P.O. Box 2028
City: Austin   State: TX   Zip: 78768

```
SUSAN YAMAMOTO                                     1767
4231 ALAMO DR.
AUSTIN, TX 78768            _____ 19___   33-57
                                                412
PAY TO THE
ORDER OF _____  $_____

_____ DOLLARS

FIRST NATIONAL BANK
OF AUSTIN, TEXAS

MEMO _____
:3455637623: 66 75 36568957 0655
```

Exercise 2

Banks in the United States open and close at different times in different places. They usually aren't open on weekends, and they are often in busy parts of the city with few parking spaces. For these reasons, many people hardly ever go into a bank to get their money from a teller. They use the drive-through window or the 24-hour automatic teller machine. You insert a plastic card in the machine, and you can get cash from your account. Most people carry a lot of plastic cards. One is for the automatic teller. The others are credit cards or "plastic money." You can buy a lot of things and pay with only one check when the monthly bill comes.

Are these sentences true [T] or false [F]?

1. ☐ Banks in the U.S. are usually open on weekdays.

2. ☐ Many people hardly ever go into a bank to get money.

3. ☐ To get cash from your account you insert a plastic card in the automatic teller machine.

4. ☐ Most people carry a few plastic cards.

Exercise 3

Now write answers.

1. What time do banks open in your city?
....

2. What time do they close?
....

3. Can you go to a bank on Saturday or Sunday?
....

4. Have you ever used an automatic teller machine? When?
....

5. Have you ever used a drive-through window? Where?
....

6. Do you have one or more credit cards? Which ones?
....

Language Summary

How	far	is it?	It's/They're	20 miles (away).	(distance)
	heavy	are they?		20 kilograms.	(weight)
	hot			20° Centigrade.	(temperature)
	high			20 meters (high).	(height)
	long			20 meters (long).	(length)
	old			20 (years old).	(age)
	wide			20 meters (wide).	(width)
	deep			20 meters (deep).	(depth)

Look at this:

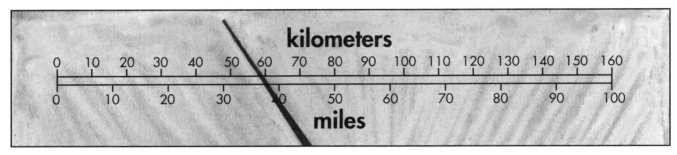

Exercise 1

100 miles = *160 kilometers*

1. 50 miles = ...

2. 120 kilometers = ...

3. 100 kilometers = ...

4. 10 miles = ...

5. 150 kilometers = ...

6. 20 miles = ...

Look at this:

World airline distances and average travel times

		Tokyo	Rome	Rio de Janeiro	Paris	New York	Mexico City
Rome	km	9,886					
	hrs	20					
Rio de Janeiro	km	18,741	9,184				
	hrs	30 ½	12				
Paris	km	9,978	1,107	9,168			
	hrs	18	2	12			
New York	km	10,990	6,888	7,751	5,839		
	hrs	16	9	10	6		
Mexico City	km	11,319	10,245	7,538	9,196	3,357	
	hrs	16 ½	15	12	12	5 ½	
London	km	10,017	1,436	9,382	336	5,562	8,919
	hrs	19	2 ½	13 ½	1	7	15 ½

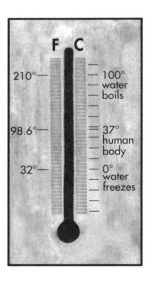

Exercise 2

How far is it from New York to Rio de Janeiro? It's 7,751 kilometers.

Write six questions and answers.

1. ....

2. ....

3. ....

4. ....

5. ....

6. ....

How long does it take to fly from New York to Rio de Janeiro?
About ten hours.

Write six questions and answers.

1. ....

2. ....

3. ....

4. ....

5. ....

6. ....

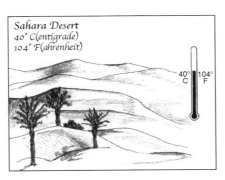

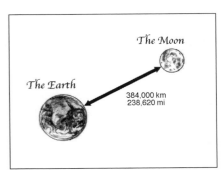

How high is Mt. Everest?
Continue.

1. ....

2. ....

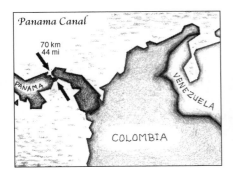

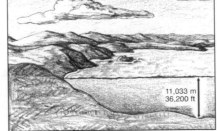

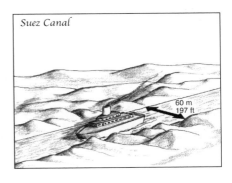

3. ....

4. ....

5. ....

Match a question from Column A with a question from Column B.

Column A
How high is it?
How deep is it?
How wide is it?
How hot is it?
How long is it?
How far is it?

Column B
What's the temperature?
What's the height?
What's the distance?
What's the depth?
What's the width?
What's the length?

Unit 20

Language Summary

I You We They	drive drove	slowly. quickly. carefully. carelessly. well.
He She	drives drove	badly. fast.

I You We They	drive drove	more slowly/slower more quickly/quicker more carefully more carelessly better	than	them. us. her. him. you. me.
He She	drives drove	worse faster		

Look at this:

He's a slow driver.
He drives slowly.
He drives more slowly than me.

She's a good driver.
She drives well.
She drives better than me.

Exercise 1

He drives quickly. (I)
He drives more quickly than me.

1. She types slowly. (he)

....

2. They play tennis well. (we)

....

3. You walk fast. (she)

....

4. I type badly. (he)

....

5. He rides his bike carelessly. (I)

....

6. She drives dangerously. (she)

....

7. He works carefully. (I)

....

8. They speak Spanish slowly and clearly. (we)

....

9. You work hard. (they)

....

Exercise 2

This is an advertisement from the *Evening News*. Two people, Rachel Chin and Fred O'Neil, have applied for the job. Helen Hughes, the sales manager of the company, has made some notes about them.

hard   *Fred works harder than Rachel.*

Write six more sentences. You can use these words:
careful/fast/clear/good/slow/late.

1. ....

2. ....

3. ....

4. ....

5. ....

6. ....

JOB OPPORTUNITIES

Sales Representative for an international company, to work in Puerto Rico, Dominican Republic, and Martinique. Must be able to type well, write clear reports, and have driver's license and credit cards (to rent car in each place). Call (616) 381-2430 for appointment.

NAME	Rachel Chin	Fred O'Neil
1 WORK (Present job)	5 days a week 7 hours a day	6 days a week 8 hours a day
2 DRIVING	no accidents	3 accidents in 2 years
3 TYPING	50 words per minute	40 words per minute
4 WRITING STYLE (English)	not well organized; not very clear	very clear and organized
5 FRENCH	good; studied 4 years in high school and college	excellent; lived in France 1 year
6 SPANISH	not wonderful; speaks slowly	bad; very, very slow
7 CREDIT	always pays on time	often pays late

Unit 21

Look at this:

bring—brought—brought   ring—rang—rung   forget—forgot—forgotten

Exercise 1

Complete these.

1. catch ....
2. .... got ....
3. .... left
4. marry ....
5. .... wore ....
6. .... took ....

7. .... found ....
8. .... lost
9. .... made
10. win ....
11. .... eaten
12. go ....

Exercise 2

Look at the example. Complete these.

A. *She walks to work every day.*
B. *She walked to work yesterday.*
C. *She'll walk to work tomorrow.*
D. *She's walked to work for two years.*

1. **A.** He can't come to work today.
   B. .... yesterday.
   C. .... tomorrow.
   D. .... for a week.

2. **A.** .... every week.
   B. He wrote to his mother last week.
   C. .... next week.
   D. .... a lot of letters.

3. **A.** .... this morning.
   B. He had to get up early yesterday.
   C. .... tomorrow.
   D. .... for three weeks.

Exercise 3

Look at this article from the sports page of a newspaper.

BURROWS WINS THREE!

INDIANAPOLIS, May 19. Lee Burrows does everything in style. Tonight he won three events in the National Track and Field Competition. He is the first person to do this since Carl Lewis in 1982. In the process, he made the world's second-longest jump (8.83 meters) and ran the world's second-fastest 200-meter race (19.45 seconds).

On Wednesday night, Burrows won the 100-meter sprint. This is the third year in a row that he has won this race. This afternoon, he won the long jump (also for the third year) and tonight he won the 200 meters. In all three events, he competed against Olympic-level athletes.

Burrows is 20 years old, 6 feet 3 inches, and 185 pounds. He comes from Tucson, Arizona. He is a student at the University of Kansas, and he is attending summer school there. He won't be able to see Indianapolis this weekend. He has to study for his economics final exam on Monday!

Now write answers to these questions.

1. How far did Burrows jump?
   ....

2. How fast did he run the 200-meter race?
   ....

3. What has he won three years in a row?
   ....

4. What events did he win in Indianapolis?
   ....

5. Who did he compete against?
   ....

6. How old is Burrows?
   ....

7. How tall is he?
   ....

8. How much does he weigh?
   ....

9. Where does he come from?
   ....

10. Why won't he be able to see Indianapolis?
    ....

Unit 22

Language Summary

It's Howard Smith, isn't it?
You're from New York, aren't you?
You aren't a secretary, are you?
You went to high school, didn't you?
You didn't go to college, did you?

You can speak English, can't you?
You can't speak Arabic, can you?
You've been to Miami, haven't you?
You haven't been to Paris, have you?

Exercise 1

You can swim, *can't you?*
Now fill in the blanks.

1. You haven't finished the course, ... ?
2. You're a student, ... ?
3. You aren't a teacher, ... ?
4. You came to class last week, ... ?
5. You didn't come on Sunday, ... ?
6. You can't speak Swahili, ... ?
7. You can speak English, ... ?
8. You're tired, ... ?
9. You're going to London, ... ?
10. You don't like this exercise, ... ?

Exercise 2

Now you are applying for a job. Fill out this application form.

```
┌─────────────────────────────────────────────┐
│   ▞▚   International Export, Inc.             │
│   ▚▞        Job Application Form              │
│                                              │
│  Job _____        │
│  Last Name _____ First Name _____   │
│  Address _____       │
│                                              │
│                 Education                    │
│  High School _____       │
│                                              │
│  College _____       │
│                                              │
│              Work Experience                 │
│  _____         │
│  _____         │
│  _____         │
│  _____         │
│                                              │
│  Languages_____         │
│  Signature _____ Date _____     │
└─────────────────────────────────────────────┘
```

Exercise 3

Look at this:

ROBBERY REPORT PD4-1/84

VICTIM

Name (Last, First, Middle Initial)	Telephone
Cowley, Sarah V.	(205) 477-8050

Address (Street, City, State, ZIP)	Sex	Age
428 Prator Road, Winfield, AL 36021	☐M ☒F	34

ROBBERY

Car	Liscense No.	State	Registration No.	Location
	386 PLJ	Alabama	3468 238177	☐Parking Lot ☒Street ☐Other
	Year	Make	Model	Color	Locked?
	1994	Chevrolet	Lumina	Metallic gray	☒Yes ☐No

Date	Time	Place/address
Oct.31	Between 7 & 9 p.m.	North St. near Perry St.

Details

I parked my car on North Street outside the Big Check
Supermarket. I locked the doors, and I went to the Ritz
Theater around the corner on Perry St. The movie started at
7:10. When I got back to the parking space, the car wasn't
there. I called the police at 9:20 p.m.

REPORT

Date	Police Officer	Victim's Signature
Oct. 31	George W. Moore	*S.V. Cowley*

It's a Chevrolet, *isn't it?*

Now fill in the blanks.

Police Officer: Well, Ms. Cowley, this is your report, ... ?
Ms. Cowley: That's right.

Police Officer: You made the report to Officer Moore last night. I just want to check the information, OK?
Ms. Cowley: Of course.
Police Officer: Now, you're Sarah V. Cowley, ... ?
Ms. Cowley: Yes, I am.
Police Officer: Your car is a 1994 Chevrolet Lumina, ... ?
Ms. Cowley: That's correct.
Police Officer: And it's metallic gray, ... ?
Ms. Cowley: Yes, it is.
Police Officer: The license number is Alabama 386 BLJ, ... ?
Ms. Cowley: No, it's ....
Police Officer: Oh, yes. I'm sorry. You parked it on North Street, ... ?
Ms. Cowley: Yes, I did.
Police Officer: And you locked the car, ... ?
Ms. Cowley: Of course. I always lock it.
Police Officer: Yes, of course. Now, you went to the movies, ... ?
Ms. Cowley: Yes.
Police Officer: Now, when you returned to the car, you didn't find it, ... ?
Ms. Cowley: No, it wasn't there.
Police Officer: Well, that seems correct. We'll call you tomorrow. The car is insured, ... ?
Ms. Cowley: Yes, it is.

Unit 23

Language Summary

I/He/She	was	working	when	I/he/she	heard the news.
We/You/They	were	watching TV		we/you/they	saw it on TV.

It was hard, but I managed to pass.

In November 1963, someone shot President John F. Kennedy when he was visiting Dallas. He died later in a hospital. The police caught Lee Harvey Oswald. Jack Ruby, a nightclub owner, killed Oswald at the police station.

November 22, 1963 was one of the most important days in modern American history. Most Americans can remember what they were doing when they heard the news of Kennedy's assassination.

Name	Age in 1963	What were you doing?	How did you hear the news?
Craig	10	Playing in the yard.	My father told me.
Betty	21	Working.	My boss told everybody in the office.
Jim	25	Watching television.	I saw it on the news.
Louise	18	Driving.	I heard it on the radio.
Mr. & Mrs. Hammond	about 35	Having coffee.	A neighbor told us.
Tony and Dave	20	Working in the factory.	We heard the news on the radio.

Exercise 1

What was Craig doing? He was playing in the yard when his father told him.

Now write five questions and answers.

1. ....
....
....

2. ....
....
....

3. ....
....
....

4. ....
....
....

5. ....
....
....

Exercise 2

How old was Craig in 1963? He was ten.

Write five questions and answers.

1. ....
....

2. ....
....

3. ....
....

4. ....
....

5. ....
....

Exercise 3

It was very hard, but the helicopter rescued them.
It was very hard, but the helicopter managed to rescue them.

Continue.

1. The ship was leaving, but I got on it.

....

2. It was nearly impossible, but the police officer rescued her.

....

3. She was very sick. The doctor saved her.

....

Unit 24 (Review)

Look at this:

Writing an informal letter.

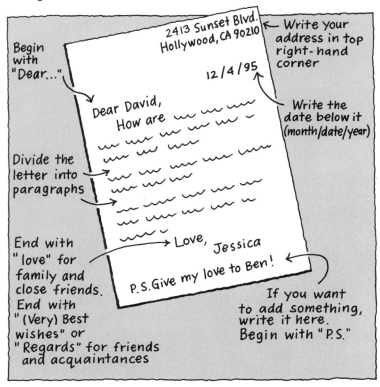

Exercise 1

My father died ten years ago.   *I'm afraid (that) my father died ten years ago.*

1. I won't be able to come to the party.

....

2. John's in the hospital. He had an accident last week.

....

3. I wasn't able to do my homework.

....

4. We can only stay in Japan for a week.

....

Exercise 2

I can call you Ollie, *can't I?*

1. That'll be nice, ... ?

2. You're from Michigan, ... ?

3. You went to London last year, ... ?

4. You haven't been to Haiti, ... ?

5. You aren't Japanese, ... ?

6. We can stay with you, ... ?

7. You've been to New York, ... ?

8. You can't speak Portuguese, ... ?

Exercise 3

Match these beginnings and endings of sentences.

I enclose a photo of Hiram and me	so they'll be able to spend Christmas together.
Ollie has a car	so he can't eat fish, meat, fruit, or vegetables.
They'll be in England in December	so you'll be able to recognize us.
Hiram will be tired after the flight	so he won't need to have dinner tonight.
Hiram is on a special diet	so he won't be able to drive.
Tom has already eaten	so he'll be able to drive Aunt Minnie around Britain.

Unit 25

Language Summary

May I see	your ticket?
	the contents of your pockets?

Look at this:

FLIGHT INFORMATION						
Destination	**Airline**	**Flight**	**Gate**	**Depart**	**Arrive**	**Aircraft**
CARACAS	Viasa	801	9	4:00 PM	8:35 PM today	DC10
LIMA	Avianca	023	15	1:00 PM	10:15 PM today	DC10
MADRID	Iberia	952	6	7:00 PM	7:45 AM tomorrow	747
RIO DE JANEIRO	Varig	861	2	8:00 PM	6:20 AM tomorrow	747
TOKYO	JAL	005	11	1:30 PM	4:10 PM tomorrow	Airbus

Exercise 1

Look at this conversation.

A: *Can I check in here for the Viasa flight to Caracas?*
B: *Yes, ma'am. That's flight 801. May I see your ticket and passport?*
A: *Sure. There you go.*
B: *That's fine. Window or aisle seat?*
A: *Oh, aisle please.*
B: *OK. Seat 17C. Here's your boarding pass. We'll call the flight in half an hour.*

VIASA
VENEZUELAN INTERNATIONAL AIRWAYS

Boarding Pass

Flight	801	
Gate	9	
Row / Seat	17 / C	
Special Diet	Yes	No X

Now write a conversation. Mr. Randolph is going to Tokyo.

A: ....
....
B: ....
....
A: ....

B: ....
....
A: ....
B: ....

Exercise 2

Paul Green is at the Varig counter.

A: *Excuse me, I'd like some information about the Varig flight to Rio.*
B: *Certainly. It's flight 861, leaving at eight o'clock tonight.*
A: *And when does it arrive?*
B: *At 6:20 AM local time tomorrow.*
A: *And what kind of airplane is it?*
B: *It's a 747.*

Mrs. Karlinski is asking about a flight to Lima. Write the conversation.

A: ....
....
B: ....
A: ....
B: ....
A: ....
B: ....

Ms. Melotti is asking about a flight to Madrid. Write the conversation.

A: ....

B: ....

A: ....

B: ....

A: ....

B: ....

Exercise 3

AIRLINE	Global	Air South
FLIGHT NO.	179	251
DESTINATION	Caracas	Atlanta
ALTITUDE	33,000 ft	35,000 ft
SPEED	500 m.p.h.	570 m.p.h.
TIME REMAINING	3 1/2 hrs.	2 hrs.
ARRIVAL (local time)	1:20	1:46
TEMPERATURE AT DESTINATION	87°F	85°F
NEAR	Gulf of Mexico	Atlantic Coast
LUNCH	a few minutes	about 5 minutes

Look at the Listening Appendix in the Student Book for Unit 25, Exercise 2 in the Student Book, and the information for Global, above. Then use the information for Air South to write another text.

Good morning, ladies and gentlemen. This is your captain speaking. ....

....

....

....

....

....

Exercise 4

Look at Exercise 3 above. Look at the Global flight.
Who?   *Who's speaking? The captain.*

Write six more questions and answers.

1. Which flight? ....

2. Where? ....

3. How high? ....

4. How fast? ....

5. How much time? ....

6. When? ....

Exercise 5

Put the words in the correct order to make questions.
the you case yourself did pack
Did you pack the case yourself?

1. you your do ticket have already

   ....

2. I please passport see may your

   ....

3. the are electrical there case any in items

   ....

4. do seating have you preference a

   ....

5. see pockets of contents I the may your

   ....

6. time flight does Lima the what leave to

   ....

Language Summary

I	enjoyed	myself.
You	didn't enjoy	yourself.
He		himself.
She		herself.
We		ourselves.
You		yourselves.
They		themselves.

It	turns	itself	on.
			off.

Exercise 1

turn—turned—turned

Complete these.

1. teach ....

2. .... cut ....

3. has ....

4. weigh ....

5. .... gone

6. study ....

7. .... rung

8. .... managed ....

Exercise 2

Fill in the blanks.

> Dear Jessica,
> This is a picture of the Acropolis.
> We're enjoying_____ very much in
> Greece. Yesterday on the beach,
> Robert stepped on some glass and
> cut his foot, but he didn't hurt
> _____ badly. This morning we took
> the children on a boat trip. They
> really enjoyed_____! Our hotel
> has air-conditioning. It's very noisy!
> It turns_____ on and off at
> night! Give my love to Ben. I hope
> you're both enjoying_____ at home.
> See you next week, Love, Kelly
>
> Jessica Edwards
> 1289 Glenwood Drive
> Petaluma, CA
> 94952
> USA

Exercise 3

I can type.   *Oh, did you teach yourself?*

Continue.

1. She can play the guitar.

....

2. They dance very well.

....

3. He plays the piano beautifully.

....

4. We can swim, but not very well!

....

Exercise 4

We've hurt ourselves!   *You haven't hurt yourselves badly.*

Continue.

1. He's hurt himself!

....

2. She's cut herself!

....

3. They've hurt themselves!

....

4. I've cut myself!

....

Language Summary

This (one)	's is isn't	as	good bad new big	as	that (one). those (ones).
These (ones)	are aren't				

John	has doesn't have	as	much money many friends	as	Maria.

John	speaks doesn't speak	as	well badly quickly	as	Maria.

Julio and Edna Lopez have just bought *Consumer Digest* magazine. They want to buy a freezer. Look at this information.

CONSUMER DIGEST'S PRODUCT REPORT
FREEZERS

MANUFACTURER	MODEL	PRICE	MINIMUM TEMPERATURE	HEIGHT	WIDTH	DEPTH	WEIGHT
CoolSpot	A70	$330	–9°C	900mm	500mm	600mm	76kg
Coldsnap	LA5800	$350	–10°C	950mm	600mm	620mm	85kg
Icequeen	HA 7001	$404	–12°C				

Exercise 1

The CoolSpot isn't as heavy as the Coldsnap.
Write five sentences. You can use these words: expensive/cold/high/wide/deep.

1. ....
2. ....
3. ....
4. ....
5. ....

COOLSPOT

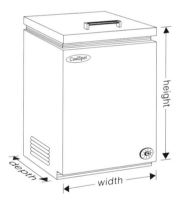

Exercise 2

He swims well.   *I don't swim as well as him.*
Continue.

1. They play tennis well. ....
2. She types fast. ....
3. He sings badly. ....
4. They work hard. ....
5. She writes carefully. ....
6. They drive carelessly. ....

Look at this:

Bob and Jackie Whitley are planning a winter skiing vacation. They have a Met Club brochure. Look at this information about two Met Club ski resorts.

Facilities	Iron Mountain, Colorado	Spud Valley, Idaho
Boutiques	10	5
Nightclubs	1	3
Restaurants	4	3
Skiing classes	10	8
Ski lifts	12	13
Doctors	3	1
Rooms	200	150

Weather		Iron Mountain, Colorado	Spud Valley, Idaho
Days with snow per season		20	26
Sunshine (number of hours per day December–March)		8 ½	9
Days with fog per season		8	15
Artificial snow necessary (days per season)		19	10
Days with rain per season		5	10

Exercise 3

Spud Valley doesn't have as many boutiques as Iron Mountain.
Write six sentences.

1. ....
2. ....
3. ....
4. ....
5. ....
6. ....

Exercise 4

Iron Mountain doesn't get as much snow as Spud Valley.
Write four sentences.

1. ....
2. ....
3. ....
4. ....

Exercise 5

Spud Valley isn't as big as Iron Mountain.
Write four sentences.

1. ....
2. ....
3. ....
4. ....

Unit 28

Language Summary

He lives in New York, doesn't he?	They weren't there, were they?	You've read that book, haven't you?
She doesn't live in New York, does she?	We were right, weren't we?	He hasn't read it, has he?
You believe me, don't you?	She was driving, wasn't she?	She was ill, wasn't she?
You don't like coffee, do you?	They weren't working, were they?	She wasn't there, was she?

Exercise 1

This is the interview with Marlene Otter.

Put in the tag questions.

Reporter: Well, Marlene—I can call you Marlene, ... ?

Marlene: Yes, of course.

Reporter: I have some information about you here, Marlene. You were born in Kingston, ... ?

Marlene: That's right.

Reporter: And you married Ben Cranshaw two years ago, ... ?

Marlene: Yes, well, two and a half years ago.

Reporter: OK. You run ten miles a day, ... ?

Marlene: Yes—but not on Sundays.

Reporter: Of course. You don't run on Sundays, ... ?

Marlene: Oh, yes I do—but only for five miles.

Reporter: Uh-huh. You're very careful about food, ... ?

Marlene: Very careful.

Reporter: You eat a lot of fish and pasta, ... ?

Marlene: Well, yes—usually, but not always!

Reporter: And Ben always travels with you, ... ?

THE SUNDAY MAGAZINE

Chicago Times, October 18

Marlene Otter—Super Athlete

Marlene Otter is one of Jamaica's most successful runners. She won five medals in the Pan-American Games last year. She trains harder than anyone. She has yogurt for breakfast, fish and salad for lunch, and pasta and salad in the evening. She was born in Kingston, and she still lives there. She was married two years ago, and her husband, the American gymnast Ben Cranshaw, always travels with her. They were in Chicago last week, and we interviewed both of them.

Marlene: Oh, yes—always!

Reporter: Great. Well, now can I ask you about your future?

Marlene: Of course. Well....

Exercise 2

Now, you're the reporter. Write ten questions for Ben Cranshaw. Use tag questions. Here is some information about him.
NOTES:
Ben Cranshaw. Born: Denver, Colorado. Studied: Georgetown University. Job: gymnast. U.S. silver medal winner, 1992. Married Marlene Otter two years ago. Lives in Kingston. Always travels with his wife. Vegetarian. Hobbies: reading. He doesn't like television. He doesn't watch it.

1. ....

2. ....

3. ....

4. ....

5. ....

6. ....

7. ....

8. ....

9. ....

10. ....

Unit 29

Language Summary

Great to see you!
Let me take your coat.
Go on in.
I like your dress.
Help yourself.

Do you want to dance?
Thanks for coming.
It was nice of you to invite me.
Thanks again.
(He was here) a second ago.

See you later.
I'm just hanging out.
Sure. Why not?

Exercise 1

Match a sentence from Column A with a sentence from Column B.

Column A
I brought some flowers.
I'm not the first, am I?
Have you had something to eat?
Do you want to dance?
Thanks for coming.
Have you seen Jack?

Column B
Yeah. He was here a second ago.
Sure, why not?
Thanks. I'll put them in some water right away.
No, not yet.
No. The others are all in the living room.
It was nice of you to invite me.

Exercise 2

Complete this conversation.

A: Hi! Great to see you. Come on in.

B: ....

A: No. The others are all here. Let me take your coat.

B: ....

....

A: Oh, thank you. I'll put it in the refrigerator right away.

Exercise 3

Put these sentences in the correct order to make a conversation.

☐ Have you had something to eat?

☐ Thanks.

☐ And there's some salad on the table.

☐ Hi, Kate. I like your dress.

☐ The snacks and cheese dip are over there…

☐ No, not yet.

☐ Thanks. It's new. I bought it yesterday.

Unit 30

Language Summary

He likes her. She likes him. .... *They like each other.*
I met you. You met me. .... *We met each other.*
Marco, you looked at Maria. Maria, you looked at Marco. .... *You looked at each other.*

Exercise 1

I understand you. You understand me.
We understand each other.
Continue.

1. He danced with her. She danced with him.

....

2. John doesn't like Mike. Mike doesn't like John.

....

3. Paul, you help Ann. Ann, you help Paul.

....

4. She believes him. He believes her.

....

5. I often write to you. You often write to me.

....

Exercise 2

Look at this:

David Bowman/Maria-Donna
How long have they known each other?
They've known each other since April.

Continue.

1. Maggie Silver/Thomas Worthington

....

....

2. Reggie Johnson/Gina Alberghetti

....

....

DAILY ECHO

☆ *Around Town* **with Kitty Kerr** ☆

All-Star Party

Last night there was a terrific party at Club Rex. *Everybody* was there. Rock star **David Bowman** was with recording star **Maria-Donna**. They met in April. The megamillionaire **Maggie Silver** of Houston and Paris was with **Thomas Worthington**, the chairman of Texxo Corporation. They met last year. **Reggie Johnson**, the baseball superstar, was with his new friend **Gina Alberghetti**. They met three weeks ago. **Dr. Ivor Sowanso** was with his wife **Dora**. They've been married for 30 years. It was a wonderful party to raise money for cancer research.

3. Ivor and Dora Sowanso

....

....

Exercise 3

My husband/wife   *We've known each other for ten years.* Write about yourself.

1. My best friend

....

2. My teacher

....

3. The student next to me

....

4. My parents

....

Exercise 4

He's looking at himself. She's looking at herself.   *They're looking at themselves.*
She's seen him. He's seen her.   *They've seen each other.*

Continue.

1. Ann hurt herself. Sonia hurt herself.

....

2. I'm looking at myself. You're looking at yourself.

....

3. Ivor's kissing Dora. Dora's kissing him, too.

....

4. I've never shouted at you. You've never shouted at me.

....

Unit 31

Language Summary

	Agreeing	Disagreeing			Agreeing	Disagreeing
I'm tired.	*So am I.*	*I'm not!*		*I'm not tired.*	*Neither am I.*	*I am!*
I've seen it.	*So have I.*	*I haven't!*		*I haven't seen it.*	*Neither have I.*	*I have!*
I like cats.	*So do I.*	*I don't!*		*I don't like cats.*	*Neither do I.*	*I do!*
I was wrong.	*So was I.*	*I wasn't!*		*I wasn't wrong.*	*Neither was I.*	*I was!*
I read it.	*So did I.*	*I didn't!*		*I didn't read it.*	*Neither did I.*	*I did!*
I can swim.	*So can I.*	*I can't!*		*I can't swim.*	*Neither can I.*	*I can!*

Exercise 1

Sara and Clara Lara are identical twins. They were born on March 19, 1970. Both of them went to Monroe College in San Antonio, and they liked mathematics. They work as computer programmers in the same office in Dallas. They usually go to Mexico for their vacation. They like Mexican food. They can't speak Spanish yet, but they are going to learn. Both of them are single. They can drive, but neither of them have cars. Neither of them are at work today because they both have colds!

	Clara	Sara
1.	I like Mexican food.	So do I.
2.	I'm not married.	....
3.	I was born on March 19, 1970.	....
4.	I can drive.	....
5.	I'm at home today.	....
6.	I went to Monroe College.	....
7.	I work in Dallas.	....
8.	I don't have a car.	....
9.	I can't speak Spanish.	....
10.	I usually go to Mexico for my vacation.	....
11.	I was in Mexico last year.	....
12.	I'm not at work today.	....
13.	I liked math at school.	....
14.	I'm going to learn Spanish.	....
15.	I have a twin sister.	....
16.	I've been to New York.	....

Exercise 2

Look at this:

Now you reply. You can agree or disagree.

1. "I'm from California." ....

2. "I don't have any friends." ....

3. "I like fruit." ....

4. "I was here last week." ....

5. "I drink a lot of cola." ....

6. "I didn't take a shower this morning." ....

7. "I brushed my teeth last night." ....

8. "I'm not a millionaire." ....

9. "I have a dog." ....

10. "I'm a vegetarian." ....

11. "I have a dictionary." ....

12. "I went to a nightclub last night." ....

13. "I didn't polish my shoes this morning." ....

14. "I don't like medicine." ....

15. "I haven't been to Chicago." ....

Unit 32

Language Summary

I'm	pleased with	it.
I was	worried about	
You're	good at	
You were	bad at	
	interested in	

I'm	sorry about	him.
I was	sorry for	her.
You're	upset with	them.
You were	rude to	
	tired of	

Look at this:

Janet Gleason has had a very interesting career. She became a doctor 15 years ago. She wrote several important books about children, and five years ago she became a politician. She's a member of Congress and often appears on television. Her grades in school weren't very good. This is her report card at the end of the tenth grade.

SIDNEY LANIER HIGH SCHOOL
Public Schools of Macon, Georgia
REPORT CARD

Name _Janet Gleason_

Grade _10_

Subject	Final Grade	Comments
English	C	A bad year. She has not been very interested in class, and I have been worried about her progress. Laura Johnson
BIOLOGY	B+	DISAPPOINTED IN HER. SHE IS VERY GOOD AT SCIENCE BUT SHE HAS NOT STUDIED MUCH. MAUREEN KONE
Geometry	A	An excellent year's work. I am very happy with her ability in geometry. Grady Dillard
World History	B—	History is not her best subject but she has tried hard. She likes history. Martin Dobrinski
Spanish I	D—	She hasn't enjoyed Spanish. She finds it difficult. I feel sorry for her. J.M. Prado
Music	D	She isn't interested in music. She is rude, difficult, and noisy in my class. Merle McCorkle

Exercise 2

Think about your report cards in school. Write sentences about yourself and your teachers.

I was interested in history and I was good at it.
My English teacher was often upset with me.

1. ....
   ....
2. ....
   ....
3. ....
   ....
4. ....

Exercise 1

A. *She was good at geometry.*
B. *Her geometry teacher was pleased with her.*

Now write sentences about Janet, and her teachers.

1. **A.** ....
   B. ....
2. **A.** ....
   B. ....
3. **A.** ....
   B. ....
4. **A.** ....
   B. ....
5. **A.** ....
   B. ....

Exercise 3

Read this letter from Jennifer to Lee. Fill in the blanks.

Amberes 39
Zona Rosa/Mexico 5, DF

Dear Lee,

Well, how are you? I'm a little worried .... my Spanish. I'm very .... in it, but I'm not very good .... it. I'm .... at speaking, but I'm not very .... at writing. Also, I'm very tired .... going to school every day. My teacher is usually very nice, but yesterday I didn't do my homework, and he was .... with me. Oh, well, I feel .... for him. It's my fault — I'm not a very good student! I'll write again soon.

Love,
Jennifer

Unit 33

Language Summary

Yes	No	?
That's right.	*That's wrong.*	*I don't know.*
That's correct.	*That isn't correct.*	*I'm not sure.*
Of course.	*Of course not.*	*I'm not certain.*
That's true.	*That isn't true.*	
I agree.	*I disagree.*	

Exercise 1

Christine Russo was a competitor in the *Yes/No Contest.* She's a teacher from Portland, Maine. She isn't married. She has one brother and two sisters. She drives a Ford Mustang. Tennis is her favorite sport. She didn't say "Yes" or "No," and she won a prize.

Write her answers to the questions.

Barry Smiles: Now, it's Mrs. Russo, isn't it?

Christine: ....

Barry: Oh, sorry. Can I call you "Christine"?

Christine: ....

Barry: Thank you. Now, you're from Portland, Oregon, aren't you?

Christine: ....

Barry: And you work in a hospital, don't you?

Christine: ....

Barry: Did you say "No"?

Christine: ....

Barry: Do you have any brothers and sisters?

Christine: ....

Barry: Oh, two brothers and one sister.

Christine: ....

Barry: Do you have a car?

Christine: ....

Barry: Did you say a "Ford Escort"?

Christine: ....

Barry: What do you do in your free time?

Christine: ....

Barry: Oh, do you like tennis?

Christine: ....

Barry: *(Buzz!)* Oh! That's it, Christine! You've won tonight's jackpot prize—a videocassette recorder!

Exercise 2

A: I went to the movies.
B: *You did?*

A: We have three cars.
B: *You have?/You do?*

Continue.

1. A: I like it very much.
   B: ....

2. A: I was born in Canada.
   B: ....

3. A: I have a cold.
   B: ....

4. A: He has three sisters.
   B: ....

5. A: She often goes there.
   B: ....

6. A: It was late yesterday.
   B: ....

7. A: I can play the guitar.
   B: ....

8. A: I'll be at work tomorrow.
   B: ....

Exercise 3

Look at this example.
TTTNONCESA...CONTESTANT

Now do the same. All the words are nouns and they are all in the Student Book between Unit 25 and Unit 32.

1. REEFPECREN ....

2. ANUCMNETENON..

3. YARVNANIESR...

4. SOLIDFGH ....

5. TUMPREOC...

6. TRANSAREUT ....

7. LAGVETEBE ....

8. RUSEN ....

9. TANCIVAO ....

10. KNEEWED ....

Unit 34

Language Summary

I	used to	do that.		Did	they	use to	do that?
He	never used to				you		
We	didn't use to				she		

Exercise 1

Dave Monsky is visiting Middleburg on business. He was born there and lived there until he was 18. He's 42 now, and he's on a street near his old home. Everything has changed. He's thinking about the past.

That video store used to be a bookstore.

Write four sentences.

1. ....

2. ....

3. ....

4. ....

Exercise 2

There's a big nightclub now. There never used to be a nightclub.

Write four sentences.

1. ....
2. ....
3. ....
4. ....

Exercise 3

Movies **A:** *Where did he use to see movies?*
        B: *He used to see them at the "Roxy."*

Now write questions and answers.

1. **A:** ....
      ....

   B: ....
      ....

2. **A:** ....
      ....

   B: ....
      ....

3. **A:** ....
      ....

   B: ....
      ....

4. **A:** ....
      ....

   B: ....
      ....

5. **A:** ....
      ....

   B: ....
      ....

Have breakfast with my friends.

Get the groceries every Friday.

Do the laundry for my mother.

Buy doughnuts.

See movies.

Buy books for my mother.

Exercise 4

Write down five things <u>you</u> used to do (and don't do anymore).

1. ....
2. ....
3. ....
4. ....
5. ....

Language Summary

Ask	him	to not to	go.		He	asked told	him	to not to	go.		He She	says thinks knows hopes is afraid is sorry is sure	he she	can can't	go.

Exercise 1

Look at this conversation.

A: International Computers. Mr. Powell's office.

B: Is Mr. Powell there?

A: No, I'm afraid he's out. Can I take a message?

B: Yes. Just tell him Jack Field called—oh, and ask him to call me tonight at home.

A: Does he have your number?

B: Yes, I'm sure he has it.

Now complete these phone messages.

1. A: Hello.

   B: Oh, hi. Is Jenny in?

   A: No, I'm sorry. She's out. This is Helen. Could I take a message?

   B: Yes. Just tell her Liz called, and could you ask her to call me back after five o'clock?

```
To: _____
WHILE YOU WERE OUT  on _____ at _____
                             date          time
M _____
From: _____
Phone No.: _____
   ☐ Telephoned        ☐ Please Call
   ☐ Came to see you    ☐ Will call back
   ☐ Wants to see you   ☑ URGENT
   ☐ Returned your call
Message _____
_____
_____
                              Operator
```

```
MESSAGE
TO: Mr. Powell              DATE: 10/20
FROM: Jack Field            TIME: 2 p.m.
OF: _____          ☑ TELEPHONED
PHONE: (    ) _____ EXT. __  ☐ RETURNED YOUR CALL
MESSAGE: Call him at home   ☑ PLEASE CALL
   tonight                  ☐ WILL CALL AGAIN
_____       ☐ CAME TO SEE YOU
_____       ☐ WANTS TO SEE YOU
SIGNED: Janice              ☐ URGENT
```

2. A: Good morning. Bradford Insurance.

   B: Is this Mrs. Henderson's office?

   A: Yes, but she isn't here. This is Mr. Rogers, her assistant. Would you like to leave a message?

   B: Yes, OK. Could you tell her Mr. Williams called, and ask her to send me an application form? Send it to 43 Dumbarton Road, Aberdeen, Maryland. The ZIP is 21001. Thanks.

```
For _____
Date _____ Time _____
          WHILE YOU WERE OUT
M _____
From _____
Phone No. _____
   ☐ TELEPHONED        ☐ URGENT
   ☐ PLEASE CALL       ☐ WANTS TO SEE YOU
   ☐ WILL CALL AGAIN   ☐ CAME TO SEE YOU
   ☐ RETURNED YOUR CALL
MESSAGE _____
_____
_____
                              Operator
```

Exercise 2

Look at the example in Exercise 1.

A: *What did Janice ask Mr. Powell to do?*

B: *She asked him to call Jack Field tonight at home.*

Now write questions and answers about the other two messages.

1. A: ....

   B: ....

2. A: ....

   B: ....

Exercise 3

He often calls his girlfriend.   *Tell him not to call his girlfriend.*

Continue.

1. He often types carelessly.

....

2. They often come late.

....

3. She often goes home early.

....

4. He often makes mistakes.

....

Unit 36

Look at these people.

Florence Hunt Smith
Age 82
U.S. Senator, 1960–91

Jacques Lebron
Age 66
Professional hockey player,
Bruisers, 1955–68

Esther O. Selznof
Age 80
Movie producer, 1940–93

I used to be a U.S. Senator.

1. ....
....

2. ....
....

3. ....
....

4. ....
....

5. ....
....

6. ....
....

7. ....
....

I used to be a professional hockey player.

1. ....
....

2. ....
....

3. ....
....

4. ....
....

5. ....
....

6. ....
....

7. ....
....

I used to be a movie producer.

1. ....
....

2. ....
....

3. ....
....

4. ....
....

5. ....
....

6. ....
....

7. ....
....

Now look at these sentences. Read **all** of them carefully. There are 21 sentences. Put them in the correct columns.

I used to score a lot of goals.	I used to practice every day.
I always used to have a secretary.	I used to work with a lot of famous movie stars.
I used to live in Hollywood, California.	I used to know all the famous politicians.
I used to work in Washington, D.C.	I used to make commercials for razor blades.
I used to wear a uniform.	I often used to wear ice skates.
I used to play for the Bruisers.	I used to meet with the president.
I used to ride in a studio limousine.	I used to be the captain of my team.
I often used to shake hands with people.	I often used to kiss babies.
I used to make speeches.	I sometimes used to get upset with actors.
I sometimes used to work in Europe.	I used to answer a lot of letters.
I used to employ a lot of people.	

Language Summary

I'm bored.	It's boring.	It bores me.
He's interested.	It's interesting.	It interests him.
She's worried.	It's worrying.	It worries her.
We're shocked.	It's shocking.	It shocks us.
You're annoyed.	It's annoying.	It annoys you.
They're frightened.	It's frightening.	It frightens them.
I'm amused.	It's amusing.	It amuses me.
He's embarrassed.	It's embarrassing.	It embarrasses him.
She's terrified.	It's terrifying.	It terrifies her.
We're excited.	It's exciting.	It excites us.
You're disturbed.	It's disturbing.	It disturbs you.

Exercise 1

Look at this questionnaire.

Opinion Research, Inc.

Questionnaire on selected prime time programs on MBS, Channel 4,
Middleburg, Week: _Feb. 6-12_
Name(s) & age(s): _Ryan (49) and Sue (43) Harris_

Program	Comments
Sunday, 8 PM SUNDAY NIGHT MOVIE "The Golden Moment" with Diana Rich.	A very nice love story. S. Too slow. Not enough action. R.
Monday, 7 PM MONDAY NIGHT FOOTBALL	The best game of the season S. I didn't see much; I was reading a book. R.
Tuesday, 8 PM MBS REPORTS Homelessness. Young people living on the streets.	The situation is very bad. The number of homeless young people is disturbing. S. and R.
Wednesday, 9 PM FOUR'S A CROWD Situation comedy.	Very funny. S. Too much bad language. Not suitable for children. R.
Thursday, 9 PM MIAMI CRIME A mugging, a robbery, a killing, a kidnapping, etc.	Too violent. I felt sick. S. Very violent, but very good. R.
Friday, 9 PM NEXT-DOOR NEIGHBORS Another episode in the lives of an Australian family.	Ho-hum. I fell asleep. S. Excellent. I enjoyed every minute. R.
Saturday, 8 PM AT THE MOVIES "Horror in Space" with Michelle Piper.	I love horror movies, but it was very frightening. S. I had a nightmare after the movie. R.

Exercise 2

What do you think of…
Horror movies? *They bore me.*
Write true answers.

1. Science-fiction movies?

....

2. Special news programs?

....

3. Police dramas?

....

4. Quiz shows?

....

5. Situation comedies?

....

6. Football games on TV?

....

The Golden Moment
Sue was: ☐ frightened ☐ bored ☑ interested
She thought it was interesting.
Continue.

The Golden Moment
1. Ryan was: ☐ bored ☐ shocked ☐ amused

....

Monday Night Football
2. Ryan was: ☐ bored ☐ interested ☐ excited

....

3. Sue was: ☐ bored ☐ amused ☐ excited

....

MBS Reports
4. They were: ☐ terrified ☐ disturbed ☐ embarrassed

....

Four's a Crowd
5. Ryan was: ☐ shocked ☐ amused ☐ frightened

....

6. Sue was: ☐ interested ☐ amused ☐ embarrassed

....

Miami Crime
7. Ryan was: ☐ worried ☐ interested ☐ amused

....

8. Sue was: ☐ terrified ☐ disturbed ☐ bored

....

Next-Door Neighbors
9. Ryan was: ☐ interested ☐ worried ☐ bored

....

10. Sue was: ☐ excited ☐ bored ☐ embarrassed

....

Horror in Space
11. Ryan was: ☐ terrified ☐ frightened ☐ interested

....

12. Sue was: ☐ frightened ☐ worried ☐ amused

....

Unit 38

Language Summary

I/you/he/she/we/they	should shouldn't should not	do that.

Should | I | do that?

Yes, you should.
No, you shouldn't.

Exercise 1

I WANT TO LEARN ENGLISH.

What should he do? Write three sentences.

1. ....
2. ....
3. ....

Exercise 2

I ALWAYS HAVE A TOOTHACHE.

A. *She should go to the dentist.*
B. *She shouldn't eat candy.*

I'M GOING FOR AN INTERVIEW FOR A JOB IN A BANK.

1. **A.** ....
....
B. ....
....

2. **A.** ....
....
B. ....
....

I'D LIKE TO PLAY PROFESSIONAL FOOTBALL.

3. **A.** ....
....
B. ....
....

I CAN'T SLEEP.

4. **A.** ....
....
B. ....
....

Exercise 3

Maybe Paul should become an auto mechanic.

Write sentences about the other students, using these possible jobs: electrician/doctor/architect/salesperson in a boutique/veterinarian/actor.

1. ....
2. ....
3. ....
4. ....
5. ....
6. ....

CAREER GUIDANCE OFFICE
Sidney Lanier High School
Public Schools of Macon, Georgia

Grade: _10_   Homeroom: _Mrs. Brandt Rm. 312_

Student:	Notes:
Abbot, Lucy	Good at math and art.
Barkoff, Paul	Very interested in cars. Good with his hands.
Thi Truong, Hoa	Excellent at biology, chemistry, and physics.
Ibarra, Raul	A fast reader. Excellent at drama.
Johnson, Sam	Interested in clothes and fashion.
Ching, Helen	Likes animals. Good at biology.
Scalese, Tony	Very good at metalwork and physics.

Unit 39

Language Summary

It's	the one	that	does that.	They're	the ones	that	do that.
He's				We're			
She's							
That's							

Exercise 1

One of them fixes cars.
One of them reports the news.
One of them works in a hospital.
One of them climbs mountains.
One of them directs traffic.

One of them works in a kitchen.
One of them works on a cruise ship.
One of them paints pictures.
One of them manages a bank.
One of them teaches ESL.

She's the one that directs traffic.

1. ....

2. ....

3. ....

4. ....
....

5. ....
....

6. ....
....

7. ....
....

8. ....
....

9. ....
....

Exercise 2

General Motors is the company that makes cars.

Write five sentences.

1. ....

2. ....

3. ....

4. ....

5. ....

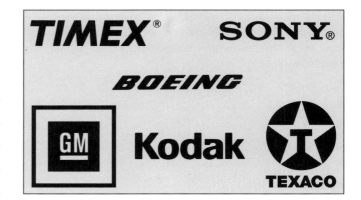

Unit 40

Language Summary

How long	have	you we they	been	doing that?		I You We They	've have	been doing that	for	two years. three days.
	has	he she							since	1988. Monday.
						He She It	's has			

Look at this hotel register. Today is July 18, and all of the guests are still at the hotel.

SEARCY INN, NANTUCKET
REGISTER

NAME	ADDRESS	ARRIVE	DEPART
Jerry Streisen	551 Columbus Ave. Apt. 4A Boston, MA 02118	7/11	
J. P. O'BRIEN	741 WEST MOOR LANE NEW DORP, NY 10306	7/12	
Carol & Nate Ackerman	3215 Q St. NW Washington, DC 20016	7/13	
Mr. + Mrs. David Shaw	2250 North Street Fairfield, CT 06430	7/14	
Paula Chandler	32 Johnson Rd. Lowell, MA 02154	7/15	
John Carter	167 Woodley Rd. Cleveland, Ohio 44101	7/16	
Heather Hillman	2857 Bankhead St. Apt. 4A Montgomery, AL 36043	7/17	

JULY

S	M	T	W	T	F	S
				1	2	3	4
5	6	7	8	9	10	11
12	13	14	15	16	17	18
19	20	21	22	23	24	25
26	27	28	29	30	31	

Jerry Streisen

A. *He arrived on Saturday.*
B. *How long has he been staying there?*
C. *He's been staying there since Saturday.*
D. *He's been staying there for seven days.*

Now write sentences about the other guests.

Paula Chandler

A. ....

B. ....

C. ....

D. ....

J. Patrick O'Brien

A. ....

B. ....

C. ....

D. ....

Carol & Nate Ackerman

A. ....

B. ....

C. ....

D. ....

John Carter

A. ....

B. ....

C. ....

D. ....

Heather Hillman

A. ....

B. ....

C. ....

D. ....

Mr. & Mrs. Shaw

A. ....

B. ....

C. ....

D. ....

Review

Read through Units 1–40 in the Student Book, and answer these questions.

Unit

1. Where does Ms. Wilson work? ....

2. What number is Paula Sinewski calling? ....

3. How much does a cup of coffee cost at the laundromat? ....

4. What is at 2.30 meters? ....

5. What train will Nick be on? ....

6. Who always cooks dinner? ....

7. What'll Waldo and Betty do about food on their voyage to Australia? ....

8. In Jackson Burns' nightmare, who rescued him? ....

9. How long will the prescription take? ....

10. What does Maria-Donna want Brandon to do? ....

11. How does the perfume smell? ....

12. Why could they take off their helmets? ....

13. Why doesn't Mike want to take a taxi? ....

14. What did Vicki have to do last night? ....

15. What has Frankie Corona never had to do? ....

16. How many times has Douglas Mackenzie taken the driving test? ....

17. What won't Jim be able to do? ....

18. Where's Ms. Akiyama's bank account? ....

19. How old is the Great Pyramid? ....

20. Why do many people dislike Natasha Terranova? ....

21. Where did Al go one afternooon last summer? ....

22. Has Paula worked in Brazil? ....

23. What were Richard and his wife doing when the earthquake began? ....

24. Where does Hiram's cousin live? ....

25. Which gate does Global Flight 179 leave from? ....

26. How long has Yolanda been married? ....

27. Why are parakeets popular? ....

28. When did the guard try to ring the alarm? ....

29. Did Kate find Bruce? ....

30. Do Rod and Kelly like each other? ....

31. Why do they never go to Miami? ....

32. Why was Caroline's father upset with Marc? ....

33. What does Richard do? ....

34. Why isn't Reggie going to play baseball again? ....

35. Where is Helen's friend working? ....

36. What was Spevna smuggling? ....

37. Is Rita's husband interested in animals? ....

38. Why can't Brian quit his job? ....

39. Who pulled a boy from a frozen lake? ....

40. How long has Vera been waiting? ....